Construction
• All flowers must be prepared before starting.
• Criss-cross all the stems in your hand as you are arranging the bouquet.
• Groupings of each type of flower can be done in the bouquet or they can be individually interspersed. If doing a grouping on one side, be sure to balance it with a smaller grouping of the same flower on the other side.
• A raffia loopy bow (see inside back cover) with long tails is tied to the bouquet to balance the bear grass on the opposite side.

Hand-Tied Bouquet

photo on page 1

Designer's Tips
• When doing hand-tied bouquets, the stems must be stripped, leaving just the very top leaves.
• When tying the bouquet with raffia, wet the raffia first (this makes it stronger).
• If a hand-tied bouquet is done well, it will stand by itself and can be displayed in a saucer-type container.

Materials
nerrine lilies
bridal pink roses
ming fern
bear grass
oncidium orchids
monte casino
white iris
calla lily
small yellow roses
10"x8½" light green ceramic container (Haeger)

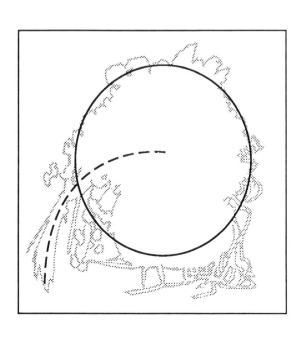

Construction

• Insert galax leaves into the foam on the right side to extend over the container edge.

• Wire some bamboo together and attach a wood pick to the center of the bamboo; insert the pick into the foam so the bamboo lies in front horizontally across the container.

• Attach two bamboo shoots loosely together with the black ribbon. Insert vertically near the back of the foam.

• Insert one phaleonopsis orchid stem into the right back of the foam to curve left.

• Bind 12 bear grass strands with the black ribbon at the base and insert into the right of the foam to extend to the right. Also bind the ends together.

• Insert a smilax garland to curve left over the container edge. Attach a 6"-8" smilax garland to a wood pick; insert at the base of the container to extend right, to the edge of the container.

• Cover any exposed foam with reindeer and sheet moss.

Orchid Stem

photo on page 4

Designer's Tip

• Binding the bear grass and the bamboo shoots together with the black ribbon brings the black of the container into the design.

Materials

galax leaves
bear grass
bamboo shoots
phaleonopsis orchid stem
smilax garland
reindeer moss
sheet moss
#1 black Bedford Bendable™ Ribbon
7"x2" round bronze ceramic container
  (Haeger)

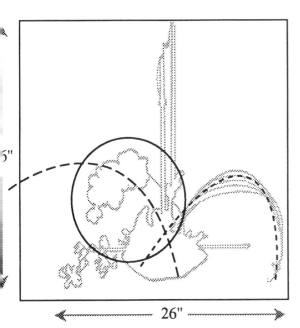

26"

3

Bunny Container
photo on page 5

Construction
• Insert three irises in a vertical line into the right side of the foam, staggering their heights.
• Insert the Scotch broom into the foam to outline the triangle shape. Insert nine yellow carnations into the bottom area of the triangle to add depth to the design.
• Insert eight yellow cushion pomps among the carnations to fill the triangle.
• Twirl some yellow ribbon along the lower right line. Insert two ribbon lengths of the yellow ribbon to two of the three irises, looping them together. Repeat with more yellow ribbon loops inserted among the carnations at the center of the piece.

Designer's Tip
• This arrangement is a triangle shape with a curved lower line to allow the bunny container to show.

Materials
irises
Scotch broom
yellow carnations
yellow cushion pomp pomps
#1 yellow Bedford Bendable™ Ribbon

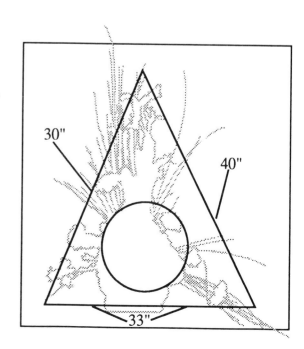

Construction

• Hot glue a piece of mauve ribbon around the edge of the container. Glue a bow (see inside back cover) with four 4" loops and no tails to the container to cover the ribbon seam. Then glue a ribbon rose (see page 34) and add curls of pink spaghetti ribbon in the bow center.
• Inside the container, add California Crystals to some water.
• Glue or wire a plush bear (ours is a mother bear holding a baby rabbit and mama is wearing bunny slippers) to a dowel and insert into the center front of the foam.
• Insert seven star gazer lilies into the foam to establish the triangular shape. Insert white liatrice to further strengthen the line. Add dried burgundy pampas grass to complete the outline.
• Insert some long springerii fern horizontally to extend the line; then add shorter stems to soften the arrangement.

Teddy Bear
photo on page 8

Designer's Tip

• The California Crystals were added to give interest to the inside of the container.

Materials

star gazer lilies
white liatrice
dried burgundy pampas grass (from Colorado Evergreen)
sprengerii fern
#9 mauve Bedford Bendable™ Ribbon
pink spaghetti Bedford Bendable™ Ribbon
#40 mauve Bedford Bendable™ Ribbon
California Crystals
dowel
stuffed animal
11"x1½" round tray

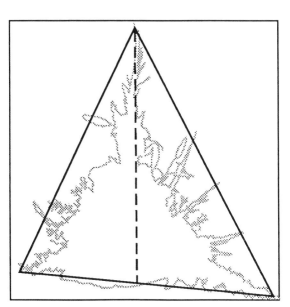

Construction

• Wrap paper ribbon spiral fashion around the basket handle, glue to secure. Repeat with the gold edged pink ribbon.

• Gather the lilies in a cluster and attach to the bottom right hand side of the basket.

• Attach some freesia clusters to the left side of the basket. Keep the freesia higher than the lilies to give good depth to the overall design.

• Intersperse some shorter sprigs of heather around the arrangement.

• Attach the corsage to the handle with a drop of pan melt glue.

Orchid Basket

photo on page 9

Designer's Tips

• Using a basket decorated with silk flowers is a wonderful idea for a permanent gift.

• When creating a design in such an unusual basket it is important that the arrangement does not hide the heart shape of the handle.

• This arrangement becomes a corsage, a flower arrangement and a decorator basket keepsake.

Materials

alstromeria lilies
heather
white freesia
a japhette orchid corsage
14"x6"x3½" moss basket
brown paper ribbon
gold-edged pink ribbon

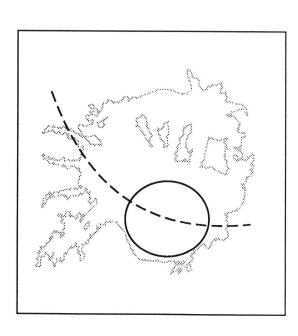

Construction

• Wrap the containers with the ribbon.
• Wrap the block of dry foam with ribbon and glue into a corner of one of the containers. Cover the top with glue and place the other container over the glue.
• Fill the bottom container with potpourri.
• Center wet foam in the upper container and insert some galax leaves around the side edges to cover it.
• Insert three gloriosa lily stems: one vertically to extend 20" above the foam, one at a 70° angle to the right 13" above the foam, and one horizontally to extend 10" to the right beyond the foam.
• Insert one 20" tall vine maple near the tallest lily and some smaller sprigs around the base.
• Frame the arrangement with 3 curly willow branches; one 20", one 16" and one 12" long.
• Cover any exposed foam with more galax leaves.

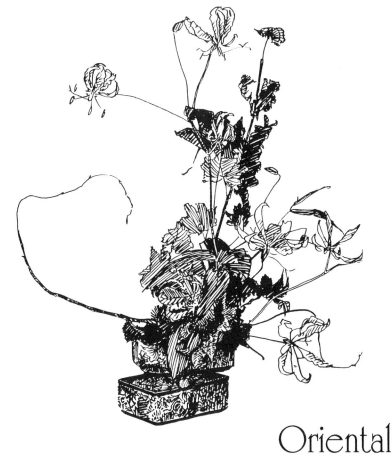

Oriental

photo on page 12

Designer's Tip

• "Framing" the design is achieved by using branches or flowers to extend beyond the edges of the arrangement. Doing this creates an area of positive or negative space which the eye perceives as part of the arrangement.

Materials

two 4"x6" black plastic containers
#9 oriental treasure Bedford
   Bendable™ Ribbon
1¹/₂"x2"x2" dry foam
potpourri
galax leaves
3 gloriosa lilies
vine maple
3 curly willow branches

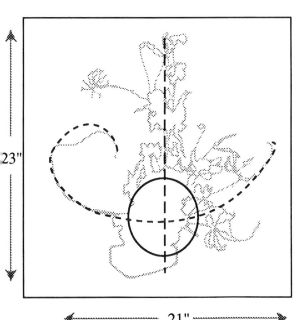

23"

21"

11

Roses in Terra Cotta

photo on page 13

Designer's Tip

• Even though a container like this would call for a Victorian design, it is totally acceptable to give it a whole different look by using a contemporary style arrangement.

Materials

4 liatrice
5 pink roses
4 stemp purple statice
2 stems button pomp pomps
4 star gazer lily buds
galax leaves
1 yard of #9 pink paper Bedford Bendable™ Ribbon
3 yards of spaghetti pink Bedford Bendable™ Ribbon
1 stem silk white lilacs

Construction

•Insert the two vertical liatrice approximately 18" and 20" above the container and then insert the two horizontal liatrice approximately 8" and 10" to the left.

• Insert the five roses with the tallest one approximately 15" and then stepping them down into the container. Make sure the tallest rose is at least 2" to the right of the liatrice.

• Insert the button pomps with the tallest one approximately 6" and stepping them down into the container. Insert the lily buds extending from the front of the container.

• Add clusters of statice, ming fern and the silk lilacs to soften the arrangement.

• Insert two tails of the #9 ribbon and bend them gently off to the right to counter balance the liatrice on the left.

• Tie a 5" loop of the spaghetti ribbon around the top of the tallest liatrice; secure it around into the vase. Add some more 5" loops into the vase.

• Cover any exposed foam with galax leaves.

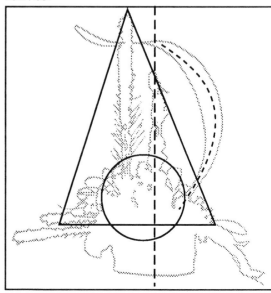

Construction

• Tuck sheet moss between the plastic liner and the basket** sides, then add the foam.

• Insert white larkspur stems in the left area. Attach some lavender spaghetti ribbon to an upper stem by bending it around the stem, then wrap the "bundle" spirally to the base. Repeat twice more.

• Insert a toothpick into the base of each brussel sprout and insert into foam in front of the larkspur.

• Insert the tulips to extend through the basket and over the right front corner edge. Insert some sprigs of ming fern among the tulips to cover the foam. Add more around the larkspur stems.

• Insert budded larkspur stems in a spray left of the bundle.

• Strip the leaves off the stems of the Jacaranda roses. Insert six in a strong vertical line to the left of the tulips. Add a grouping of six short open roses to the right of the brussel sprouts.

Spring Basket
photo on page 16

• Insert mauve dahlias keeping them lower than the handle, allowing them to bridge the two tall elements.

• Insert sprigs of heather among the tulips and larkspur buds, adding depth to both ends of the design.

Designer's Tips

• When preparing the foam, cut off the sharp upper corners, making less foam to cover and allowing softer lines.

• Interpretive bundling is when different stem lengths are bundled together resulting in a very full design.

• When working with a basket or container with holes, build the design through the holes, bringing the arrangement lower.

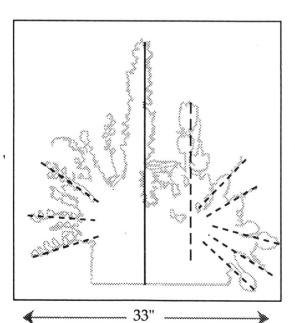

← 33" →

15

A Circle of Roses

photo on page 17

Designer's Tip
• When using bear grass, all lengths should face the same direction so they curve the same way.

Materials
white roses
oasis® igloo foam
wire
galax leaves
prayer plant leaves
bear grass
ming fern
twig globe (from Luzon)

Construction
• Glue the wet oasis® igloo to the inside bottom of the globe. Insert some galax leaves around the base of the foam, rolling the ends under to hide the foam.
• Insert four short roses into the front of the foam in a cluster inside the globe. Insert three more roses; one inside the globe and two taller ones extending out the top of the globe.
• Cut the lower 4"-12" off about 20 strands of bear grass and wire the upper ends of the lower pieces to a wood pick. Insert the pick into the lower left of the foam. Wire the lower ends of the upper pieces to another pick. Insert this into the right side of the foam, creating the look of the grass going through the foam.
• Insert sprigs of ming fern on each side of the lower roses. Also insert fern sprigs behind the roses to lightly fill the globe.
• Insert five prayer plant leaves near the bottom of the globe, three under the roses and two to the left of them.

24"

Construction

• Cut a 2" thick piece of styrofoam® to fill most of the basket and cover it with the lamé fabric and tulle. This holds the soaps and gifts up where they can be seen. Secure the gifts by gluing a wood pick to the back of each package, then inserting it through the fabric into the foam. Be sure to insert the larger packages first.

• Once all the packages are inserted and secured, attach a piece of the white lace ribbon to the basket diagonally across the top, glue the ends at the back.

• Insert the roses into the outer edges of the foam. Establish the height by making the top rose as tall as the basket is wide. Insert the mini-carnations deeper into the arrangement. Insert heather and Queen Anne's lace to fill the area of the triangle.

• Make a bow (see inside back cover) with 5" loops and 6" tails from the mauve ribbon overlaid with white lace. Attach the bow to the base of the flowers with the tails over the basket side.

• Insert a smilax garland to the left of

Gift Basket

photo on page 20

the bow to soften that corner of the basket. A very thin smilax garland is placed diagonally across the basket to further soften the whole look.

Designer's Tip

• To make gift baskets look fuller, add materials such as excelsior, shredded metallic package filler, paper raffia or Spanish moss tucked around and under the gift items.

Materials

gifts of your choice
styrofoam®
silver lamé fabric
pink tulle fabric
#9 white lace ribbon
#9 mauve ribbon
bridal pink roses
hot pink mini-carnations, heather
Queen Anne's lace
smilax garlands
white wicker basket

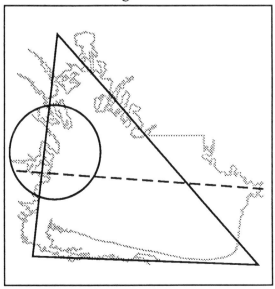

19

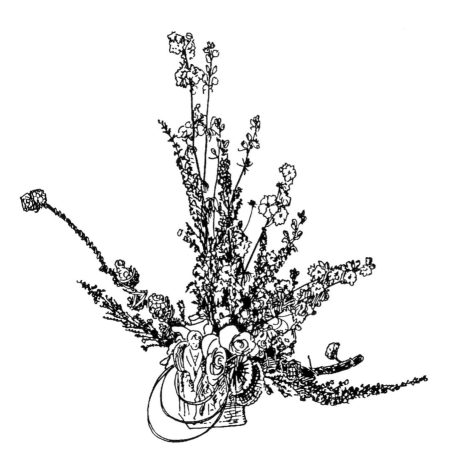

Cherub Design
photo on page 21

Designer's Tip
• The container is delicate and the branch is heavy, therefore miniature ribbon roses were glued to the branch softening it.

Materials
bridal pink roses
jack pine cone branch (Colorado
    Evergreen)
larkspur
heather
pink spaghetti Bedford Bendable™
    Ribbon
#3 pink Bedford Bendable™ Ribbon
galax leaves
16-gauge wire
3¹/₂" rectangular pink ceramic con-
    tainer

Construction
• Bind a 26" jack pine cone branch with the pink spaghetti ribbon. This brings the pink from the container up into the design.
• Insert three 3"-6" loops of pink spaghetti ribbon in a cluster to drape around cherub.
• Make a "U" shaped pin from the wire. Place the pine branch over the foam and secure it to the foam with the "U" pin.
• Make five ribbon roses (see page 34) from the #3 pink ribbon. Glue them to the branch.
• Insert 10"-20" stems of larkspur into the foam on the right establishing a triangle shape
• Insert heather to add some depth to the design and to extend the lower curve established by the pine branch.
• Insert four bridal pink roses around the cherub being careful not to hide it.
• Roll two galax leaves around your finger and insert into the foam to the right of the cherub.

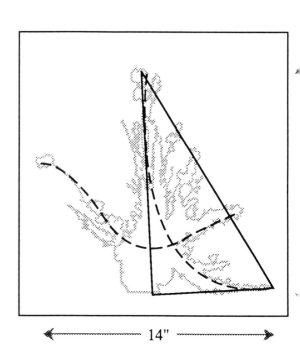

14"

Corsage Construction

• For the wristlet band: Make two 5" long loops with the gold spaghetti ribbon. To wear, slip one loop into the other and bend the ends back to secure.

• Cut off a 6" length of the gold spaghetti ribbon and set aside. With the rest of the gold ribbon, make 3"-5" loops.
• Hold the loops and add the silver spaghetti ribbon, making more 3"-5" loops.
• Tie the bow with the 6" length and intersperse the silver with the gold loops. Curl each end around a pencil.
• Shape the bow loops. Glue rose leaves to the loops as a background. Glue ming sprigs as filler radiating out from the bow center.
• Cut the orchids from their stems and glue them among the ribbon loops and fern.
• Glue two heather sprigs extending toward each end.

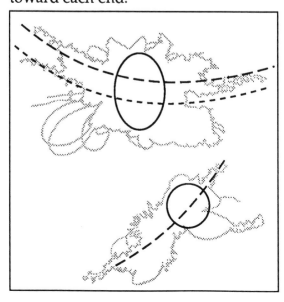

Corsage/Boutonniere

photo on page 24

Boutonniere Construction

• Cut off a 6" length of silver spaghetti ribbon. Make five loops with the silver ribbon then tie them with the 6" length. Curl the tied ends around a pencil or dowel.
• Glue the rose leaves to the loops as a background. Glue the rose in place with one heather sprig on each side of it and one angled downward. Glue the ming fern over the rose stem.
• Bring a ribbon loop around the rose.

Designer's Tips

• Flowers must be at room temperature to ensure proper gluing.
• If sprayed with a preservative, such as Crowning Glory, and stored in a cooler, this corsage and boutonniere can be made up to three days ahead.
• Use a low temperature (200°) pan melt glue to ensure against harming the fresh materials! You cannot use a hot or cool melt glue gun because the flowers will come loose in the cooler.

23

Bridal Bouquet

photo on page 25

Designer's Tip
• Dipping the roses into the Elmer's glue mixture will stop them from opening any further. This treatment can only be used on pastel colored roses.

Materials
roses
smilax garland
opalescent spaghetti Bedford
 Bendable™ Ribbon
peach tulle
pink tulle
bridal bouquet holder
Elmer's glue

Construction
• Mix five parts water with one part Elmer's glue in a jar. Dip the roses; put in a vase and let dry.
• Insert the roses in a tight mound into the foam, alternating the colors. Make sure the roses touch each other as they are inserted.
• Loop and pin 10" lengths of peach and pink tulle into the foam around the edges of the holder. Pin some long streamers into the bottom of the holder.
• Wire some ribbon loops and streamers together and pin into the bottom of the holder in front of the tulle streamers.
• Insert some long, heavy smilax garland behind the tulle; pull some strands to the front. Tuck some shorter sprigs among the roses to soften the starkness of the solid roses.
• Loop some spaghetti opalescent ribbon over the top of the roses securing the ends into the foam.

Construction

• Bundle about 20 stems of the equisitium and tie together with a wire at the base. Insert into the foam.

• Cover the foam with moistened sheet moss.

• Make concentric circles with 18" of the #40 ribbon. Glue the outside end to the outside loop. Hot glue a 3" pick to the back and insert it into the foam so it secures the ribbon circles and allows them to sit on top of the moss. Do the same with a 12" piece of the #9 ribbon and insert it into the foam.

• Cut a slit in the moss down into the foam for each rose and insert them so the bottom of the rose goes through the moss and well into the foam where its water source is.

• Attach a 17" piece of the #9 ribbon to the bottom of a wood pick and insert it into the foam behind the #40 ribbon. Bring the ribbon up to the back of the equisitium and attach with a drop of glue. Repeat with a 23" piece of ribbon and bring it up around the taller rose and attach it to the underside of the lower rose with a drop of hot glue.

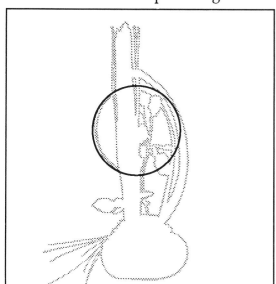

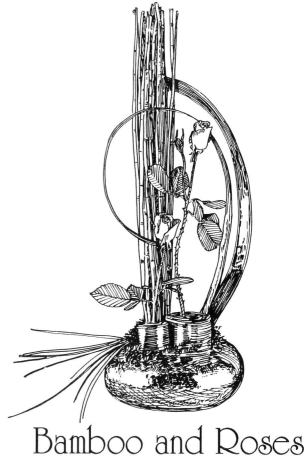

Bamboo and Roses

photo on page 28

Designer's Tip

• A simple arrangement of only two flowers can be made extraordinary when presented with flair. Use Bedford Bendable™ Ribbon to house the rose stems as well as to frame them. The use of framing in this design creates what is called negative space.

Materials

2 sonia roses
dried equisitium
sheet moss bear grass
#9 jewel copper Bedford Bendable™
  Ribbon
#40 jewel copper Bedford Bendable™
  Ribbon
glue gun and hot glue
3" wood picks

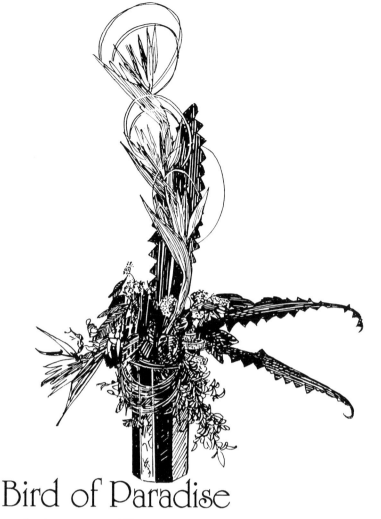

Bird of Paradise

photo on page 29

Designer's Tip
• If a bird of paradise center blossom is past its prime pick it off, then gently open the pod and ease the inside blossom out. Remove the greenish blossom casing.

Construction
• Glue #40 gold paisley Bedford Bendable™ Ribbon to opposite sides of a 4"x4"x10" black plastic vase. Repeat with #9 gold paisley Bedford Bendable™ Ribbon on the other two sides.
• Insert three birds of paradise vertically into the foam, staggering the lengths. Insert the last one horizontally on the left.
• Cut the edges of the ti leaves to make them jagged. Insert two to extend horizontally right and one vertically behind the birds of paradise. Spray the leaves with leaf gloss.

• Insert one smilax garland into the foam going over the right side of the vase, and one horizontally left. Insert galax leaves around the stems to cover the foam.
• Make a loop of black spaghetti Bedford Bendable™ Ribbon and a loop of gold spaghetti Bedford Bendable™ Ribbon. Insert into a bird of paradise blossom. Repeat for each vertical bird of paradise
• Make 15-17 loops of black spaghetti ribbon, and attach them to a wood pick. Repeat with gold spaghetti ribbon. Insert the gold loops horizontally into the foam to cascade over the edge of the foam. Insert the black loops vertically above the gold ones.
• Cut the lemons into slices. Insert two toothpicks into the foam at the base of the flowers. Insert the lemon slices onto the toothpicks in a "staircase."
• Insert two flat leaf eucalyptus branches near the back of the arrangement, one on each side of the upright flowers. Insert six prayer plant leaves around the base to cover any exposed foam or wood picks.

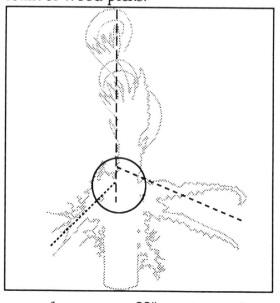

23"

Construction

• Glue the igloo foam base to the flat area of the branch. Insert galax leaves around the base of the foam to cover the sides.

• "Finger strip" two ti leaves on both sides of the center stem and one only on one side. Insert one leaf that has been stripped on both sides and one that's been stripped just on one side vertically into the foam. Insert the last leaf horizontally in front of the branch.

• Insert two stems of Connecticut King Lilies upright and one stem horizontally. Add more stems to fill the area between the first two and one around the front to form a triangular shape.

• Attach reindeer moss to cover any exposed foam.

Windswept

photo on pages 40 & 41

Designer's Tip

• To "finger strip": use your fingernail to slit the leaves, stopping before the edge. This along with the desert whalebone, gives the design a *wind-swept* look.

Materials

desert whalebone (Colorado Ever green)
Connecticut King Lilies
galax leaves
ti leaves
reindeer moss
oasis® igloo floral foam base

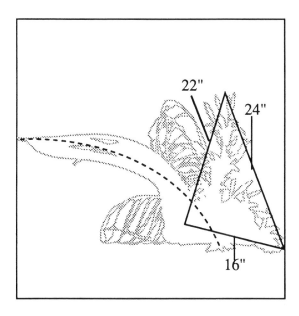

22"

24"

16"

31

FLORAL RIBBON ROSE

You will need: 1 yard of #40 Bedford Bendable™ Floral Ribbon
                       6" length of spaghetti or #1 Bedford Bendable™ Ribbon

 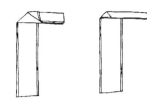 

1. Measure 5" from one end and fold it as shown. Notice the fold is on top, toward you and not behind the long piece.

2. Fold the 5" piece in half horizontally. Then fold the 5" end in half horizontally again. (Hold onto this folded end while completing the rose.)

3. Fold the left end back, then roll the right end (the rose center) toward the left.

4. Continue rolling the right end at an angle, forming a funnel shape. Fold the left end back again and roll the right end toward the left.

5. Continue folding and rolling to within 3" of the ribbon end. Bring this 3" tail under the rose and hold together with the folded end.

6. Use the 6" length of spaghetti or #1 ribbon to wrap around both ends just under the rose, securing them.

LOBSTER TAIL BRAID

You Will Need: 2 yards of ⅝" wide Bedford Bendable™ Ribbon (makes a 9" long braid)
                   4 yards of 1½" long Bedford Bendable™ Ribbon (makes an 18" long braid)

1. Fold the ribbon length in half but do not crease. Make a loop as shown.

2. Make an uncreased fold using the left ribbon with the end on top. Insert this fold through the loop. Pull the right ribbon to tighten the slip knot. Adjust the fold so it is long enough to allow another loop to be inserted.

3. Make a loop with the right ribbon, positioning the end on the bottom; insert this loop through the last loop.

4. Pull the left ribbon to tighten the slip knot.

5. Make a loop with the left ribbon, again with the end on top.

6. Insert into the previous loop. Tighten the loops. Continue in this manner to the end of the ribbon.

7. To secure the left ribbon, do not make a loop, but insert the ribbon end through the previous loop. Trim evenly with the loop.

8. To secure the right end, turn the braid over and trim the end to 2". Bend it inward and insert it into the back of the last loop.

Construction

• Cut a 1" wide slot down one side of the vase. Wrap the vase with the 9½" wide ribbon to extend 8" past each end. Lay the vase on its side; tie each end with the #1 gold ribbon. Curl the ends of the narrow ribbon around a pencil.

• Insert three galax leaves into each end to cover the foam.

For the parallel groupings: Insert three irises on the left end and four red carnations on the right end. Nine white mums are inserted around the base between the carnations and the irises with one mum outside the carnations. Insert the bear grass behind the irises, curving them to the left.

Lobster tail braid napkin rings: Make two 9" braids (see page 42) using the #3 jewel ocean blue ribbon. Form into a ring and glue to hold. Loosely wrap 18" of the gold spaghetti ribbon spiral fashion around each ring, inserting the ends among the braid to secure.

Firecracker Children's Party

photo on page 36

Designer's Tips

• When grouping bear grass, make sure all the strands face upward; then all will curve the same direction.

• If the cylinder container tends to roll, cover two bamboo lengths with ribbon and glue one on each side at the base of the cylinder.

Materials

4 red carnations
10 white mums
3 irises
bear grass
galax leaves
gold spaghetti Bedford Bendable™ Ribbon
#3 jewel ocean blue Bedford Bendable™ Ribbon
#1 gold Bedford Bendable™ Ribbon
9½" wide gold confetti Bedford Bendable™ Ribbon
3" wide plastic cylinder vase, pencil

Construction
• Glue foam into the container. Insert all the flowers into the foam.
• Attach the ming fern to cover any exposed areas of the foam.
• Wrap the branch spiral fashion with the ribbon and insert the branch into the foam to "frame" the design.

Marbelized

photo on page 37

Designer's Tip
• To marbelize your container: Fill an old bucket with water. Spray the first color of paint onto the top of the water; dip the container into the water repeatedly until the desired amount of the first color remains on the container. Spray a second color into the same water and dip the container again. Repeat with as many colors as desired. Each different color of paint can be done as heavily as you desire. Let the container dry completely and spray with sealer.

Materials
nerrine lilies
spider pomps
gladiola florets
pine cone branch
sedum, ming fern
teal spaghetti paper Bedford
  Bendable™ Ribbon
8"x8"x2¹/₂" plastic container

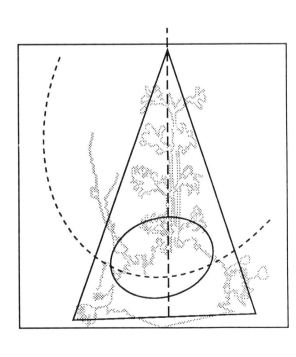

Construction
• Insert the date palm embryo upright into the foam. Insert the galax leaves to cover the sides of the foam and over the right edge of the container.
• Insert one tall and two short sunflowers under the palm.
• Insert the bear grass strands on the back right, bringing the ends around unevenly and pinning them into the foam on the left behind the lowest sunflower.
• Attach reindeer moss on the front and sheet moss on the back of the foam over the galax leaves.

Summer's End

photo on page 40

Designer's Tips
• When using something dark and dead, contrast it with something soft and vibrant.
• "Sheltering" is done by inserting a tall material to extend up and over a shorter material. In this arrangement the date palm embryo is "sheltering" or protecting the sunflowers from the hot sun.

Materials
date palm embryo (Colorado Evergreen)
sunflowers
bear grass
reindeer moss
sheet moss
galax leaves

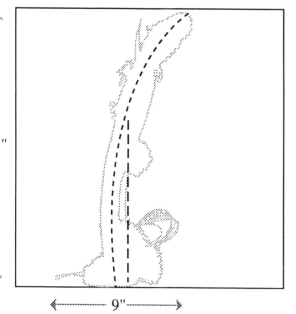

9"

Oncidium Orchids

photo on page 41

Designer's Tip
• Hana Kubari is the oriental concept of bending twigs and inserting them into the vase to hold the floral stems in place. In this interpretation, ribbon was used in place of twigs.

Materials
oncidium orchids
bear grass
#1 yellow Bedford Bendable™ Ribbon
4"x2$\frac{1}{2}$"x4$\frac{1}{2}$" glass vase

Construction
• Using the yellow ribbon, make four sets of coils by carefully lifting the ribbon off the reel to preserve the coil shape. Place the coil sets in the vase one at a time, allowing the sets to mesh together in the vase.
• Using the same technique as above, make two sets of five concentric circles, securing the ends and leaving 4" long stems on each set. Insert one into the vase angled down over the front and the other extending upward.
• Insert a 24" orchid stem vertically into the vase among the ribbon coils. Add a 21" stem angled to the left and a 17" stem angled to the right front. The circles of ribbon inside the vase will hold the stems upright.
• Insert 12 strands of bear grass angled from the back right corner of the vase. Tie the ends together in a knot.

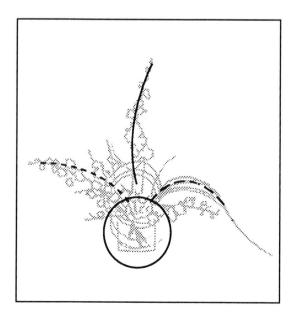

Construction

• Insert three yellow cremons upright into the center of the foam, staggering the lengths. Insert a bittersweet branch on the left side of the foam to arch over the cremons. The graceful flow of the bittersweet gently enfolds the cremons and shelters them.

• Slice the kiwi into ¼" thick pieces and dip into fruit preservative. Insert two flat edged toothpicks into the side of each slice of fruit and insert into the foam at the base of the cremons, creating two "staircases."

• Insert three warnecki dracaena leaves layered on the right side of the design, extending over the container edge. Insert flat eucalyptus and ming fern sprigs to add depth and to complete the design.

Bittersweet

photo on page 44

Designer's Tip

• This arrangement is simple and based on the curve of the container. It includes a combination of the framing (page 11) and sheltering (page 39) techniques; the bittersweet branch does both.

Materials

yellow cremons
bittersweet branch
warnecki dracaena leaves
flat eucalyptus
ming fern
kiwi
fruit preservative (Fruit Fresh™)
flat toothpicks
6"x6"x5" bronze ceramic container
   (Haeger)

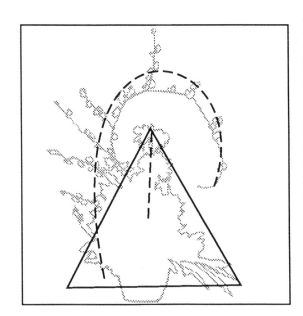

45

Thanksgiving Centerpiece

photo on page 45

Designer's Tip
• A centerpiece should be tall to be seen well. The candles provide height in this arrangement, yet allow guests to "see through" it across the table.

Construction
• Spray the candlesticks gold and cut them to varying heights; insert into the foam. Wrap #9 jewel copper Bedford Bendable™ Ribbon around the container; glue to secure.
• To ripple the #3 antique peach Bedford  Bendable™ Ribbon: Place a glue stick on the table, lay the ribbon over it. Place another glue stick on top of the ribbon next to the first stick. Slip a third stick under the ribbon next to the last stick, then add another stick on top of the ribbon next to the last one. Pull out the first stick and slip it under the ribbon. Continue to ripple the ribbon using and re-using the four glue sticks.

• Wrap #1 jewel copper Bedford Bendable™ Ribbon spiral fashion around the candlesticks; wrap it loosely around the upper portion and tightly around the lower area.
• Wrap #3 antique peach Bedford Bendable™ Ribbon spiral fashion around two candles. Add horizontal wraps on the other two candles and glue to secure.
• Insert some natural oats to tone down the glitz of the ribbon.
• Use clear gerbera stem (from Stemsons) straws and insert gerbera daisies with two in the center at the base of the candles and four radiating out from the center. Insert oncidium orchid stems among the daisies to bring out the darker colors and to brighten the arrangement.
• Insert more oats and vine maple to fill the oval shape. Add galax leaves to cover any exposed foam.
• Slide horizontal ribbon pieces up on the candles; insert a single orchid under the ribbon, slide the ribbon down to secure the flower. One orchid should be on each of the two horizontally wrapped candles.
• Tuck an orchid into one of the other candlesticks and one under the narrow ribbon on the same stick.

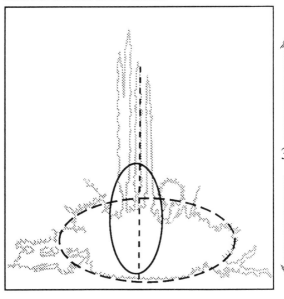

27"

Construction

- *Lightly* spray the cornucopia with gold spray paint.
- Cut a 1" wide hole in the upper area of the cornucopia. Insert some short sprigs of vine maple and one short rose into the hole. Insert longer vine maple sprigs into the lower front of the cornucopia, angled right. Add shorter vine maple sprigs in the center area of the foam.
- Insert some long eucalyptus branches to extend upright and angled out the lower area of the cornucopia. Insert shorter branches to extend out the center area.
- Glue two long wood picks to the bottom of each piece of fruit. Spray all the fruit gold; insert them at different lengths and angles among the greens in the cornucopia.
- Insert the roses and gerbera daisies to follow the lines of the arrangement and to fill the center area among the fruit.

Cornucopia Cascade

photo on page 48

Designer's Tip

- The gerbera daisy stems are inserted into clear gerbera straw stems then into the foam; this keeps them from drooping.

Materials

roses
gerbera daisy straw stems
eucalyptus
vine maple sprigs
gold spray paint
wooden pear and apple (W.J. Cowee)
clear gerbera stem straws
12"x7" wicker cornucopia

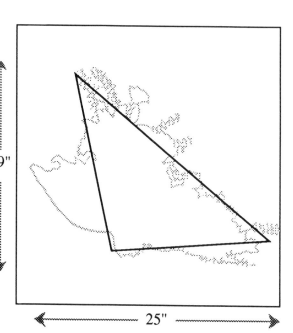

9"

25"

47

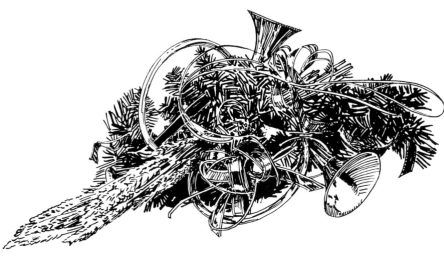

French Horns

photo on page 49

Designer's Tip

• Bedford Bendable™ Ribbon can often be used in place of different gauge wires--the biggest benefit is that you don't have to cover the wire when you use the Bedford Bendable™ Ribbon.

Materials

two 10" brass French horns
4 stems of polyvinyl Christmas greens
⅓ bunch of dried gold wheat
2 yards of #3 classic red Bedford Bendable™ Ribbon
2 yards of spaghetti classic red Bedford Bendable™ Ribbon

Construction

• Attach two stems of Christmas greens together and a piece of spaghetti ribbon overlaying them. Attach two more stems of Christmas greens with ribbon.
• Criss-cross the two wired pieces and connect the centers with the spaghetti ribbon making sure the stems are behind the greenery on the opposite side.
• Tie the two French horns to the greenery background, angling one horn upwards and the other downwards.
• Band the wheat with the #3 ribbon and attach it to the greenery, angled between the horns. Make about 12 concentric circles of spaghetti ribbon and add them to the arrangement.
• Make a bow (see inside back cover) with the #3 ribbon and attach it to the greenery as a finishing touch.

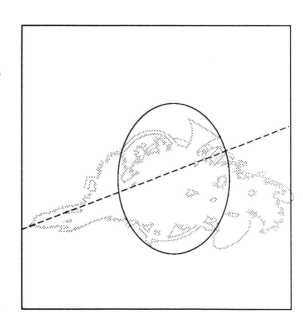

Construction

• Insert a pine branch in a gentle curve to frame the arrangement.
• Insert four roses in a vertical line at different heights. Add five more roses in a tight group at the base of the first roses.
• Insert the mauve sedum to nestle into the pine branches just left of the roses.
• Slice oranges and dip them into fruit preservative to keep them from drying out or turning color. Insert two toothpicks into each orange slice and insert in a "staircase" at the base between the sedum and roses.

Materials

9 fire roses
mauve sedum
pine branch
oranges
fruit preservative (Fruit Fresh™)
flat toothpicks
11"x11"x3" grey/black plastic marble
    container

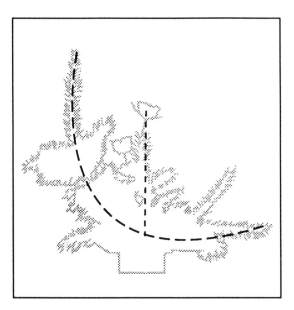

Oranges and Roses

photo on page 52

Designer's Tips

• "Framing" visually sets up an area in the arrangement for the eye to look at which is larger than the actual arrangement. It allows you to use a minimum of flowers and yet have the arrangement appear much larger.
• Inserting the oranges in a "staircase" brings your eye back down to enjoy the beauty of the container.
• An arrangement which includes citrus fruit cannot be kept in the cooler with other flowers as the fruit emits ethylene gas which damages fresh flowers. If this design is made ahead of time, very tight flowers must be used and the arrangement must be left sitting out.

White Birch Arrangement

photo on page 53

Designer's Tips
• It is important to make the shape of the arrangement open, to accent the white birch and give the arrangement an important Christmas feeling.
• To show the maximum amount of container (birch bark, in this case), cut a <u>very</u> small hole in the top of the bark, creating less space to fill.

Materials
white carnations
noble fir sprigs
white birch bark (Colorado Evergreen)
#9 red velvet Bedford Bendable™
    Ribbon
glue
6" wide plastic liner

Construction
• Insert the foam into the liner and place inside the bark. Cut a small hole in the top of the bark through which the flowers are inserted.
• Add white carnations through the hole on the top of the bark in a basic triangular shape. Insert more carnations through the opening at the front of the bark.
• Insert noble fir sprigs around the upper carnations.
• With red velvet ribbon make a bow (see inside back cover) with two long tails. Glue it to the base of the upper carnations with the tails looped to the back.
• Make two sets of one ribbon loop and a tail; wire each to a wood pick. Insert these to extend out the end of the bark.
• Glue a small curl of the bark in front of the upper stems.

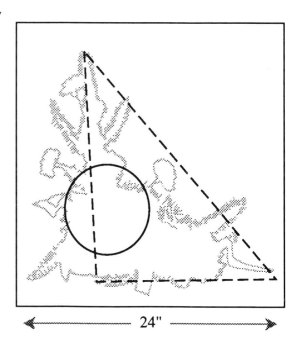

← 24" →

Construction

• Mount the igloo on the upper side of the wreath. Insert some long cedar branches into the lower edges of the igloo to extend downward. Insert shorter branches into the top to extend upward. Insert more short branches into the sides of the igloo.

• Insert Queen Anne's lace among the cedar. They contrast and soften the harsh branches of the wreath.

• Wire six streamers of the #9 red ribbon to a wood pick. Insert into the bottom left of the igloo to extend among the lower cedar branches. Four concentric circles of ribbon are tightly wired and attached to a wood pick. Then insert them into the igloo over the streamers.

• Bend each stem of four apple picks into a "U." Dip each into glue and insert into the wreath among the cedar.

• Wire five more long ribbon streamers to wood picks and insert into the bottom of the foam. Curve them to drape in "loops."

• Fill empty foam areas with fir sprigs.

Fresh Wreath

photo on page 56

Designer's Tips

• The flowers used in this design will dry naturally in the wreath.

• If kept outside, this design will remain fresh for 3-4 months.

Materials

apple picks
cedar branches
fir sprigs
Queen Anne's lace
#9 red confetti Bedford Bendable™ Ribbon
large Oasis® igloo
glue
grapevine wreath (Colorado Evergreens)

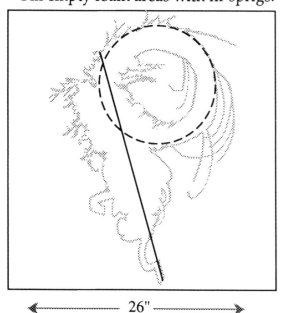

1"

← ⋯⋯⋯⋯ 26" ⋯⋯⋯⋯⋯ →

Birds and Cinnamon

photo on page 57

Designer's Tip
• When doing an artificial wreath, it is always nice to incorporate something with a fragrance. In this wreath, the cinnamon sticks were used.

Materials
cinnamon sticks
curly willow stems
gold spaghetti Bedford Bendable™ Ribbon
1⅝" wide red/gold striped ribbon
¼" wide gold picot ribbon
two birds
artificial wreath

Construction
• Lay three cinnamon sticks on the wreath and tie in place with the striped ribbon. Place two more on top and tie a half knot with the same ribbon, then place one on top and tie again securing with a square knot this time.
• Make two bows (see inside back cover) one with the striped ribbon and one with gold picot ribbon, each with four long streamers; secure each with wire. Tie the bows to the wreath over the cinnamon sticks. Loop two striped tails separately along the wreath below the sticks. Secure the loops by twisting pine sprigs around the ribbon. Loop a gold picot tail through each striped loop.
• Wire some curly willow stems angled downward across the wreath from the bow.
• Glue a bird to a branch just above the cinnamon sticks and one in the lower area of the wreath.
• Bind the thinner willow branches sporadically with gold spaghetti ribbon. Some twists will curl away from the branches, therefore attach at each ribbon end.

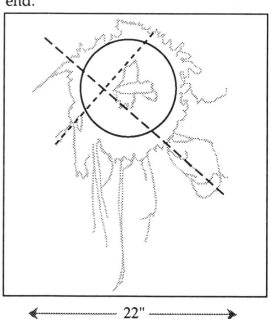

22"

Construction

• Using the green and gold stripe ribbon, wrap the container, gluing in the back to secure. Overlay with the gold paisley ribbon.

• Hold all carnation stems together and shape them into a sphere. Bind the stems with the #1 gold ribbon, criss-crossing and keeping them tight. Insert into the foam in the container.

• Cover the foam with moss. Insert an 11" evergreen sprig over the edge of the base horizontally on the right side. Insert the apple stem into the moss over the evergreen.

• On the opposite side from the first evergreen, attach an 8" evergreen stem up near the carnation blossoms.

• Using the #1 gold ribbon, make twelve 5"-7" loops and secure together, leaving a 6" stem. Insert the stem through the stems of the carnations at the top right side and wrap around several stems. Using the gold paisley ribbon, make two loops and two tails, attach them to the carnations near the evergreen sprig on the left. Secure ten 4"-6" loops of the gold ribbon and insert at the base opposite from the evergreen. Make two more loops from the

Carnation Topiary

photo on page 60

paisley ribbon each with two tails. Insert into the base between the evergreen and the gold loops. Shape the tails in ripples. Add another tail to extend among the evergreen.

Designer's Tip

• Strip all foliage off carnations before starting the project. The cleaner the stems, the nicer the vertical line of the topiary will be.

Materials

16-20 white carnations
8" apple pick with three apples
evergreen sprig
#40 green/gold stripe Bedford Bendable™ Ribbon
#9 gold paisley Bedford Bendable™ Ribbon
#1 gold Bedford Bendable™ Ribbon
reindeer moss
5½"x3" gold plastic container

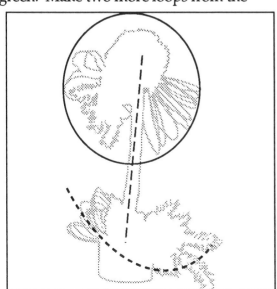

Roses and Tassles

photo on page 61

Designer's Tip
• When using roses in a cluster, as in the center of this arrangement, it is very important to have the heads of the roses at various heights. This allows a strong amount of weight at the top of the container without allowing the arrangement to be out of balance.

Materials
14 roses
3 pine stems
2 verdigris lotus pods
1 stem of variegated dendrobium orchids
peach and gold tassles
#3 antique peach Bedford Bendable™ Ribbon
5½"x2½"x8⅓" dark green ceramic container (Haeger)

Construction
• Insert three pine stems into the container to establish the triangle: one vertical and a horizontal stem extending off each side.
• Insert seven roses "stepped" up the arrangement in a very strong vertical line. To give visual weight to the container, insert an additional seven roses clustered along with two verdigris lotus pods at the base.
• Encircle the vertical line of roses by loosely wrapping them spiral fashion with the antique peach ribbon.
• Insert a single stem of variegated dendrobium orchids diagonally to give movement to the arrangement. Attach peach and gold tassles under the lotus pods to give further movement.
• Make four 3"-6" loops using the #3 ribbon and insert them among the tassles.

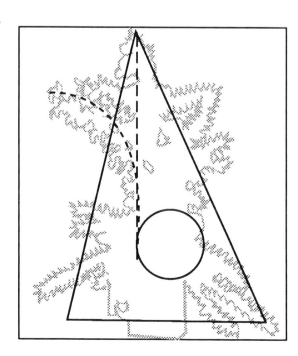

Construction
• Place the chipeta wood branch to extend to the left over the vase, wedging the other end inside to hold it in place.
• Curve one lily dramatically (see designer tips). Insert it to extend over the back edge and around through a hole in the vase.
• Gently curve the other lilies and insert them into the vase to curve over the right side.

Blue Vase

photo on page 64

Designer's Tips
• To curve calla lilies: Warm the stem and, holding both ends, gently pull the stem back and forth over your knee. Pull the ends lower as the stem curves.
• The curves and roundness of the container are duplicated in the design.

Materials
3 calla lilies
one 20" long chipeta wood branch
    (Colorado Evergreen)
dark blue ceramic pottery (Haeger)

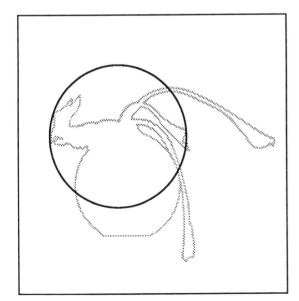

63